Learn About Books

Dinosaurs

Written by
Bobbie Whitcombe

CHECKERBOARD PRESS

NEW YORK

About 220 million years ago, the first dinosaurs lived on the Earth. The world was very different. Lands that are now separated by oceans were joined together then. In some places there were swamps. In others there were forests of huge trees. The weather was much warmer. There were no people.

brachiosaurus (brack-ee-oh-sawrus)

Dinosaur means 'terrible lizard'. Dinosaurs were reptiles, as lizards and crocodiles are today. Some of them were the biggest animals that have ever lived on land. The largest were the **brachiosaurus**. Each one probably weighed about the same as 16 elephants. Their nostrils were on top of their high-domed heads.

Most of the largest dinosaurs were gentle plant-eaters. They needed to eat a huge amount and had enormous stomachs. Some swallowed stones to help digest their food! They often lived in herds, like these **apatosaurus.** This protected them from attack by the fiercer meat-eating dinosaurs.

apatosaurus (*ap-at-oh-sawrus*)

Diplodocus was the longest dinosaur. It stretched about 27 metres (89 feet) from head to tail. Look how its long neck helped it to eat the leaves from the tops of the trees.

diplodocus (*dip-lod-oh-cus*)

Some of the dinosaurs did not eat plants.
These were the meat-eaters. They had sharp
claws and teeth. They preyed on lizards,
large insects and other dinosaurs.

tyrannosaurus rex (*ty-ran-oh-sawrus rex*)

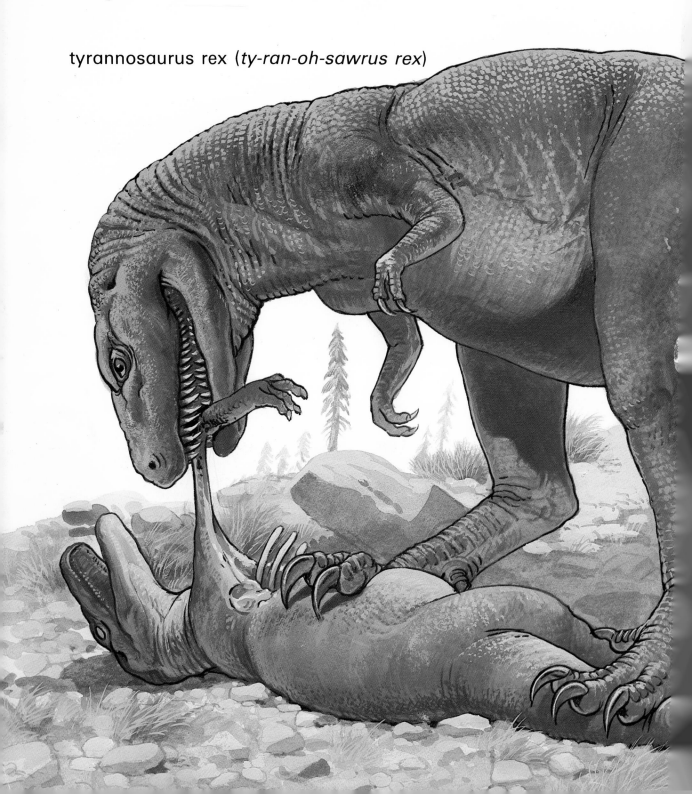

Tyrannosaurus Rex was the largest and fiercest of the meat-eating dinosaurs. It stood 6 metres (20 feet) high and moved on its back legs. It only had two fingers on each of its short arms. Each of its sharp teeth was as long as a pencil.

ankylosaurus (*an-kyle-oh-sawrus*)

The big plant-eaters moved slowly and could not easily get away from their enemies. Some of them, like the **ankylosaurus**, were protected by an armour of bony plates. Look at the hard knobby club at the end of its tail. It could swing this hard at any attackers.

Stegosaurus could grow up to 9 metres (29 feet) long. It too had a dangerous tail. Those sharp spikes would keep most enemies away. It also had two rows of bony plates along its back. These may have been for defence. They would also have helped the creature to take in heat if it turned sideways to the sun.

stegosaurus (*steg-oh-sawrus*)

triceratops (*try-sair-oh-tops*)

Some dinosaurs had a frill of bone around their heads and horns on their faces. They had strong mouths like beaks and flat teeth for chewing the toughest of plants. The biggest of these was the **triceratops**, which had three horns. These protected it from its enemies.

Styracosaurus was another horned dinosaur. Its name means 'spiky lizard'. It was 6 metres (20 feet) long and it weighed about 4,000 kg (8,800 pounds). The horn on its nose was 70 centimetres (over 2 feet) long.

styracosaurus (*sty-rak-oh-sawrus*)

If attacked, these dinosaurs would point their horns forward and charge with all the force of their enormous weight behind them.

pachycephalosaurus (*packy-sefa-loh-sawrus*)

Pachycephalosaurus means 'thick-headed lizard'. The heads of these dinosaurs had a dome of solid bone 25 centimetres (10 inches) thick. They probably fought each other with their heads to decide who was to be leader of the herd.

Look at the long bony
crest which **parasaurolophus**
had on the back of its
head. Its jaws looked
like a duck's beak.
Inside its mouth were
hundreds of small sharp
teeth. It used them to
eat leaves. When it
stood up, it was as
tall as a giraffe.

parasaurolophus (*para-sor-ol-oh-fus*)

At the same time as the dinosaurs, giant reptiles swam in the seas. **Plesiosaurs** were up to 13 metres (42 feet) long. They ate mainly fish. With their powerful flippers, they could swim backwards as well as forwards. **Ichthyosaur** means 'fish lizard'. Ichthyosaurs were good swimmers. They ate fish and shellfish, which they crushed with their long snouts and sharp teeth.

plesiosaurs (*pless-e-oh-saws*)

ichthyosaurs (*ik-thee-oh-saws*)

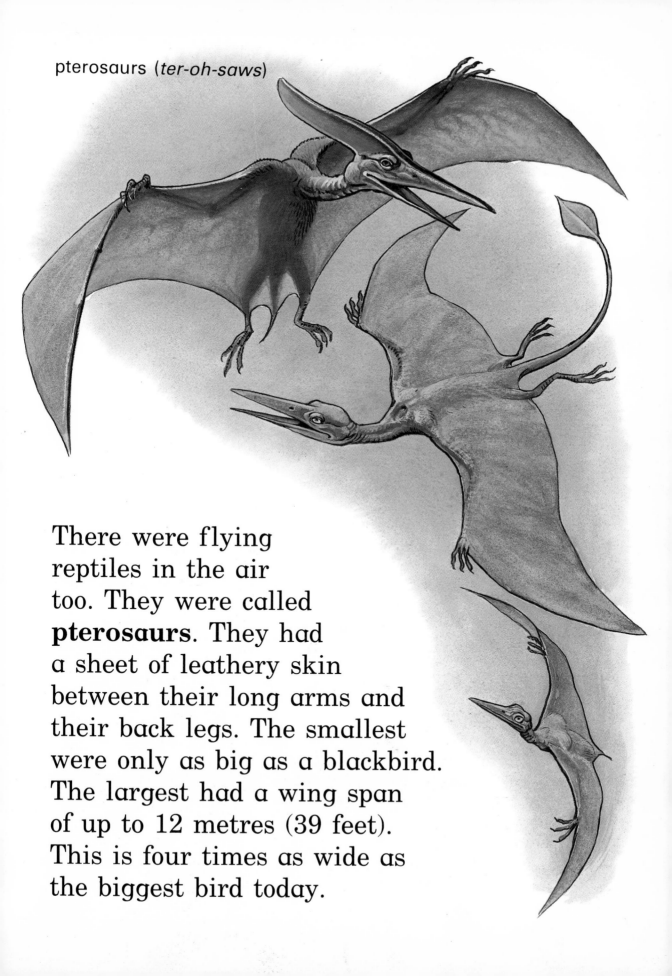

pterosaurs (*ter-oh-saws*)

There were flying
reptiles in the air
too. They were called
pterosaurs. They had
a sheet of leathery skin
between their long arms and
their back legs. The smallest
were only as big as a blackbird.
The largest had a wing span
of up to 12 metres (39 feet).
This is four times as wide as
the biggest bird today.

There are no dinosaurs alive today, but their bones can still be found. When some of these creatures died their bodies fell into muddy rivers or the sea. Over many years, the mud or sand built up and hardened into rock. The bones then became fossils. Some fossils are found when the rock splits or if it is worn away by rain and wind.

Sometimes people find fossils when they dig in mines or quarries. The bones are carefully cleaned and fitted together to show people what the creature looked like. You can see dinosaur skeletons in museums.

The age of the rocks in which fossils are found tells us how long ago the creatures lived. Fossil records show that the dinosaurs disappeared from the earth about 65 million years ago. The giant flying and swimming reptiles died out, too. Why did this happen at that time?

Probably it is because over thousands of years the earth had become colder. The dinosaurs could not eat enough to keep their bodies warm and had no fur or feathers to keep the heat in. When the plant-eaters died out, the meat-eaters grew short of food. So the dinosaurs became extinct.

Now you have read about many different dinosaurs. Can you recognise these ones?

apatosaurus
plesiosaur
stegosaurus
ankylosaurus
diplodocus
triceratops